CW01467287

Becoming Vegan

The Beginner's Guide to Vegan Cooking

Includes Vegan Cooking Basics, Stocking Your Vegan Pantry, Replacement Vegan Ingredients, and 10 Vegan Recipes

CAC Publishing
ISBN: 978-1-948489-18-8
Brittany Boykin

Table of Contents

Introduction

What is Vegan cooking?

Nowadays, our modern society is concerned with various issues. Our health is one of the issues at the very forefront. People want to eat well and be healthy.

Many of us have decided to make the health-conscious choice to become Vegan.

Simply put, Vegan cooking is food which is prepared within the Vegan qualifications so that it supports that way of life.

What does it mean to be Vegan?

Vegan is a subdivision of vegetarianism, and there are a number of different categories of Vegans. Some vegetarians still drink milk and/or eat eggs. Vegans don't. Vegans are the most stringent and they do not want ANY animal products in their diet.

It can be very challenging, since most of the time people take many things for granted. Eggs and milk, for instance, are commonly used baking ingredients. Thus, replacements need to be made if a Vegan is going to eat baked goods.

So, how do you know your foods are Vegan?

Food must adhere to a certain criteria in order for it to be considered strictly Vegan. Note that there are many hidden ingredients in most foods. It is particularly vital that you watch out for these ingredients if you are going to attempt a Vegan diet.

- ✓ Vegans do not ever eat any animal products or byproducts of animal products.
- ✓ Vegans do not eat things such as milk and eggs.
- ✓ Vegans do not eat fish.
- ✓ It is important to remember that bees are an animal. Therefore, Vegans also do not eat honey, royal jelly, or bee pollen supplements.
- ✓ There are plenty of other hidden ingredients to watch out for which make their way into our food including gelatin, lard, and whey.

If you are a beginner, making these changes can be quite overwhelming at first, but after you have been eating and cooking the Vegan way for a few months, you will become a pro.

What This Book Will Cover

If you are reading this book, you probably know that a vegetarian diet, chiefly a Vegan one, can be fantastic for your health. Many people are all about improving their health, hence the popularity of health food stores has become huge. This makes it much easier to enjoy a nourishing Vegan diet. This book sets out to teach you how to do that by showing you:

- ➢ The fundamentals of cooking Vegan food the correct way.
- ➢ An outline of typical ingredients used in Vegan cooking.
- ➢ A list of hidden ingredients which you want to avoid while eating a Vegan diet.
- ➢ Information on how to stock a wide-ranging Vegan pantry so that you can make Vegan dishes every day without the hassle.
- ➢ Basic cooking methods to create an assortment of satisfying meals.
- ➢ How to create a complete Vegan meal and still receive the correct balance of vitamins, minerals, and nutrients.
- ➢ How to handle special nutritional needs like diabetes or high cholesterol.

➢ Great recipes to get you started right away.

There is so much great information to learn while striving to enjoy a Vegan diet. This book is intended to teach you everything you need to know.

Chapter 1: Classic Ingredients in Vegan Cooking

Vegan cooking is done without meat, fish, eggs, or any byproducts. In order to maintain a Vegan way of life, added care should be taken to ensure that none of these ingredients end up in your food.

When cooking, we tend to take certain things for granted, like using eggs when baking. Eggs are not permitted on a Vegan diet. And, although the Vegan way of life is growing in popularity, pre-packaged Vegan food is still hard to come by. Therefore, many Vegans choose to do their own cooking instead.

Chapter 1 will concentrate on a number of different kinds of ingredients. First, we will learn how to replace the milk and eggs with other ingredients which are Vegan friendly. We will also cover info on additional ingredients which are commonly used and also animal byproducts to watch out for.

Replacing Eggs in Your Recipes

Replacing eggs in our Vegan recipes can be quite a challenge. In fact, eggs are one of the hardest ingredients to substitute. Though, there are alternatives to choose from.

What are the eggs for in recipes anyway?

In most recipes, eggs are important as they bind the ingredients together. They are also used to make baked goods rise and help to make your baked good light and fluffy. In addition, they help to form structure and provide added moisture. Eggs are particularly useful when baking, but they are also necessary for certain savory dishes as well.

Options for Egg Replacement

Below is a list of the best egg replacement options. You can use these options to replace the eggs in any recipe:

Pureed Bananas

Pureed bananas are effective as an egg substitute. Simply put a ripe banana in the blender and pulse till totally smooth with no lumps. Half of a regular banana is equal to one egg.

Nevertheless, bananas have a distinct taste which doesn't always work out in all recipes. For instance, if you were making peanut butter cookies, the banana flavor would change the taste.

Ground Flaxseeds

You can purchase already-ground flaxseeds. However, it is better to buy flaxseeds whole and keep them in the refrigerator. When you are ready to use them, measure out 1 tablespoon for every egg that you need to substitute. Then, pulverize your flaxseed it in a blender or coffee grinder.

Transfer your flaxseed to a bowl and add 3 tablespoons of water for each egg you need to substitute. Add water gradually while whisking vigorously. Whisk the mixture until it takes on a gel-like quality.

Because flaxseeds have a nutty taste, this egg substitute works best when preparing recipes such as whole grain breads, muffins or pancakes. You can always experiment and decide which recipes you like to use this replacement in.

Egg Replacement Product

There are a number of egg substitutes on the market which are designed to be Vegan friendly. Always be sure to inspect the packaging and be sure that your product is Vegan safe and also does not contain any meat byproducts.

These substitutes are in the form of powders, and they get mixed reviews. Some like them a lot, others not at all. They are, though, convenient and good to have on hand. Once you get used to cooking Vegan, you will learn which foods taste best with these powders.

Because there are quite a few brands available, it might take a while to find the one that you're happy with. As far as using, just follow the package instructions. You can purchase these egg substitutes either at the health food store or online.

Tofu

Tofu is an alternative choice you can try. Try any form of tofu that you would like, however this may take some experimentation. It seems that silken tofu yields the best results. And, you can also use unflavored soy yogurt with similar results.

The good thing about tofu is that it balances well with most flavors. Tofu does not really have much flavor and is perfect especially when combined with stronger ingredients. And, it is commonly available in most health food stores and regular supermarkets.

Simply blend the tofu until smooth in the blender. You can also use a food processor, but it's important to ensure that there are no lumps and is as smooth as possible. To substitute one large egg, use ¼ cup of the blended tofu.

You'll need to do some experimenting to see which recipes work best with tofu as an egg substitute. Experiment to find which recipes taste best with the tofu. It all depends personal preference.

Flour and Other Leavening Agents

Another option is using pastes made from different kinds of flours and leavening agents as an egg substitute. Most of you will have these ingredients on hand. They also don't have a flavor and they blend into the batter fairly well.

Here are some options:

> ➤ 1 tablespoon of flour - any kind (wheat flour, oat flour, or soy flour work well) with 1 tablespoon water for each egg.

> ➤ 1 tablespoon baking powder, 1 tablespoon flour, 2 tablespoons water for each egg.

> ➤ 2 tablespoons corn starch and 2 tablespoons water blended together also replaces one egg.

Finding the Right Egg Substitute

Once more, as you attempt these different blends, you will learn which egg replacements work best for which recipes. As a recommendation, you might want to begin with one of your favorite foods and try different egg substitutes until the flavor and texture you want are achieved.

For instance, if you want to prepare blueberry muffins, you can substitute the eggs for any one of the above substitutions. Note how it tastes. Next time, try a different substitute. After trying a few, decide which one was your favorite and stick with it. Before long, you will know automatically which egg replacement works best for which recipes.

Replacing Milk in Your Recipes

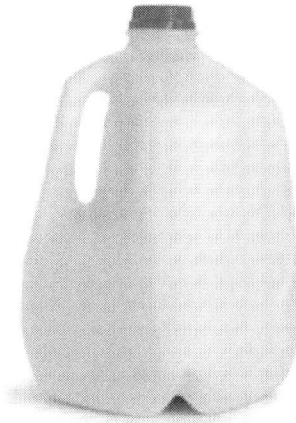

If you become a true Vegan, milk from any animal (sheep, cow, goat, etc.) is not allowed. Milk is also a very common ingredient when baking and cooking. However, it is much easier to substitute than eggs.

To substitute milk in recipes, use any of the below Vegan alternatives. For instance, if the recipe calls for one cup of milk, use one cup of soy milk in its place. Here are the alternate milk options:

> **Soy milk**
> Soy milk is readily available and comes in a variety of flavors which includes vanilla, unsweetened, chocolate, and even egg nog. Some brands are thicker and creamier than others. Like above, you will need to experiment so you can find the brands

you like the best. Unless it has a distinct flavor, soy milk is fairly neutral and blends well in recipes. Soy milk is also rich in protein and helps to keep you feel full for longer.

> ➢ **Nut milks**

Nut milk beverages like almond milk or hazelnut milk are also options. Unlike soy milk, nut milks have a distinctive flavor and might not work well in all recipes. Nut milks come in sweetened and unsweetened varieties.

> ➢ **Rice milk**

Rice milk is also a great option to replace milk. It is mild and blends well. Though, you may want to note that rice milk does not have a lot of protein, so you might need to compensate for that.

> ➢ **Coconut milk**

Coconut milk is a plant product, a white liquid extracted from coconut. It has nothing to do with animals and can be used as a safe Vegan substitute.

As you test the different flavors of these milk replacements, you will get acquainted with which recipes will taste best with them.

Replacing Buttermilk

Buttermilk is another ingredient used in numerous recipes. A Vegan cannot use traditional buttermilk because it is an animal product. Buttermilk is basically regular milk which has been cultured, meaning it has good bacteria in it much like yogurt.

Fortunately, you can simply make your own. The method is as follows, and it creates one cup of Vegan-friendly "buttermilk".

1. Put 1 tablespoon of lime juice, lemon juice, white vinegar, or apple cider vinegar into a measuring cup.

2. Add non-dairy milk until it reaches the 1-cup line; stir with a fork or whisk.

3. Allow mixture to sit for 5-10 minutes.

Soy milk works the best.

Replacing Butter and Lard

Butter is an ingredient that a lot of recipes call for. There are quite a few different things you can do to substitute it:

➢ **Vegetable oil**

If your recipe calls for melted or solid butter, you can use vegetable oil in its place. Vegetable oil can sometimes change the consistency of the recipe a little, so you will undoubtedly have to experiment.

➢ **Shortening**

If you require the use of a solid fat, you can use Vegan-friendly shortening. However, shortening is a manufactured product and filled with trans fats. So you may want to use it in moderation. You can also find butter-flavored shortening when a butter flavor is vital.

> **Margarine**

Margarine is yet another option which can replace butter or other solid fats. Margarine is especially good if you want that buttery flavor. Yet, margarine is also high in trans fatty acids.

> **Reducing Fat**

It is also possible to reduce fat with fruit purees. For instance, if your recipe calls for 1 cup of butter, you can instead use ½ cup apple sauce and ½ cup Vegan margarine or shortening. You can also use plum puree and banana puree. You can sometimes find fruit puree fat replacement products at the market, but you want to make sure they are Vegan friendly. You can also replace all of the fat in the recipe with fruit. Just keep in mind that for some people this option may alter the texture too much.

Make sure that butter replacement products are used in moderation. A diet which is high in fat and trans fats is not a healthy diet.

Common Ingredients Used in Vegan Cooking

Without a doubt, Vegan cooking is an art. As we learned above, ingredients like milk, buttermilk, eggs, and butter are <u>almost</u> indispensable in certain recipes. Nevertheless, the substitutions we discussed are more than sufficient. Having said that, there are numerous ingredients that Vegan chefs find vital. Below are some of the most common.

Soy Products

Soy is perhaps the most useful, particularly when it comes to making healthy and protein-rich Vegan dishes. Here is a list of some of the soy products you will want to keep on hand:

- ✓ **Soy milk**

  Soy milk is readily available and can be found in several different flavors.

- ✓ **Tofu**

  Tofu is sold in different levels of firmness such as extra firm, or soft.

- ✓ **Tempeh**

  Tempeh is a fermented product with a robust, meaty

consistency which can be used in stir fry and other dishes.

✓ **Ground Meat Replacement**

Ground meat replacement is a soy food and is a staple to many because you can use it to create meals such as Spaghetti Bolognese and Vegan chili.

✓ **Soy Yogurt**

Soy yogurt contains active cultures just like regular yogurt and is sold in a variety of flavors.

✓ **Miso**

Miso is a fermented salty paste which is made from soy and is used as a common enzyme-rich soup base.

✓ **Tamari and Soy Sauce**

Tamari and Soy Sauce are both condiments which are made from soy.

✓ **Edamame**

Edamame are fresh soy beans and are superb by themselves or in stir fry.

✓ **Soy Cheese**

Soy cheese melts and has a similar consistency as real cheese.

✓ **Soy Sausage, Hot Dogs, and Hamburger Patties**

Vegans can enjoy breakfast sausage, hot dogs, and even hamburger patties made with soy.

✓ **Soy Chicken**

Soy chicken comes in a variety of forms such as patties, nuggets, etc.

✓ **Soy Protein Powder**

Soy protein powder is a great way to increase your daily protein consumption. You can put a scoop in your smoothie, or add it to recipes like pancakes and breads.

✓ **Soy Flour**

Soy flour is a valuable product, chiefly for baking.

There are an assortment of soy products to choose from apart from those listed above. See out soy products which are made from non-genetically modified soy beans.

As with everything, soy has its critics. Some Vegans only use soy products in its "traditional" forms like tofu, tempeh, miso, Edamame, and tamari. Opponents of processed soy products are wary of the fact that they are designed to taste like meat or milk products. This, to them, defeats the purpose of being Vegan. And, they tend to be highly processed which does not necessarily make them healthier. Whether or not you decide to use these soy products is totally up to you and your journey.

Whole Grains

There are so many different types of whole grains. Grains are rich in vitamins, minerals, fiber, and added nutrients, including protein, and quinoa – an ancient grain that is rich in protein. Below you will find some whole grain products that will be great in your Vegan lifestyle:

- ✓ Rye
- ✓ Buckwheat
- ✓ Quinoa
- ✓ Wheat products
- ✓ Pasta
- ✓ Brown rice
- ✓ Oats

These grains can be ground into flour or used whole. They are essential for a healthy Vegan diet.

Nuts and Seeds

Nuts and seeds are another vital part of a healthy Vegan diet. They are rich in vitamins, minerals and important nutrients such as like healthy fats. Below is a list of nuts and seeds that are great for your diet:

- ✓ Hazelnuts (filberts)
- ✓ Walnuts
- ✓ Sunflower seeds
- ✓ Pumpkin seeds
- ✓ Pecans
- ✓ Almonds
- ✓ Cashews
- ✓ Sesame seeds
- ✓ Poppy seeds
- ✓ Flax seeds
- ✓ Hemp seeds

They are great in recipes or as a snack.

Legumes

Legumes are an important protein source for a Vegan, particularly when combined with whole grains. They should be combined to form a complete protein.

Below are some examples of legumes:

- ✓ Chick peas (garbanzo beans)
- ✓ Lentils
- ✓ Kidney beans
- ✓ Black beans
- ✓ Cannelloni beans
- ✓ Northern beans
- ✓ Black eyed peas
- ✓ Split peas

Legumes are available in dried form, ground into flour, or canned. The dried form must be soaked overnight to soften it. The canned form is easy to use and great to have on hand. The flour is also a popular ingredient in baked goods and flavorful cooking.

Fruits and Vegetables

Essential for good health, fruits and vegetables enhance your food with color and variety. As a Vegan, your complete diet will be plant based, so it is important to obtain your vitamins, minerals, and nutrients from food like fruits and vegetables.

Seek out organic produce when possible as it is the healthiest.

Seasonal local produce is best. It helps support your local economy and tastes a lot fresher.

Canned and Pre-Packaged Foods

Now that the Vegan diet is increasing in popularity, so does the accessibility of pre-packaged, Vegan-friendly foods. Below are some of the things you can find:

- ✓ Breads
- ✓ Desserts
- ✓ Baked goods
- ✓ Snacks
- ✓ Vegan chocolate
- ✓ Canned goods
- ✓ Beverages
- ✓ Breakfast foods and cereals

And even better, most of the time you won't even have to go to a health food store to find a lot of these products. Health food stores are a great option for buying Vegan products, but you can find a lot of Vegan products in your regular supermarket.

Hidden Ingredients to Look Out For

As mentioned above, there are often hidden animal byproduct ingredients in foods. A true Vegan must take the added step to examine these ingredients and avoid them. If you purchase a pre-packaged food that is listed as being Vegan friendly, you can be fairly confident that it does not have these ingredients. However, when just starting out, it is still a good idea to check until you have learned what is good and what is not.

Below is a list of the ingredients to be careful for. There are 2 kinds of ingredients, the ones that are clearly from animal products, and the ones that might be from animal products or might be from plant-derived products.

In the second category, the only way to truly find out is by communicating with the manufacturer of the food product by either phone or email. If they don't know, it's safe to say that you should not purchase the product.

Hidden Ingredients from Animals

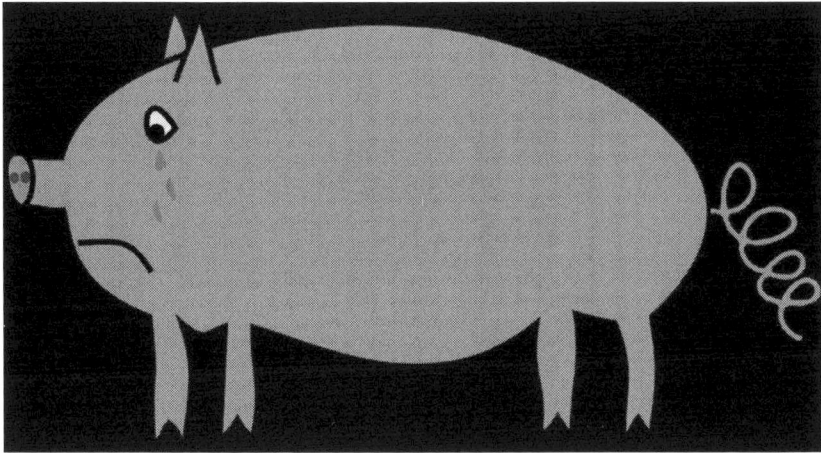

The below ingredients are pretty common in foods. Unless a product is labeled as Vegan, you really should inspect the ingredients list carefully to ensure that they are not included.

- ➢ **Albumin** - comes from egg whites

- ➢ **Milk products -** includes whey protein powder, lactase, lactose, and things like milk and dried milk

- ➢ **Calcium Caseinate** – a fairly common additive

- ➢ **Calcium Stearate** – also another additive

- ➢ **Suet** – a type of animal fat

➢ **Tallow** – animal fat product is made from suet

➢ **Bee products** – This includes royal jelly, propolis, honey, and bee pollen

➢ **Carmine** – a food additive that comes from insects

➢ **Lard** – a type of animal fat

➢ **Casein** – this is the protein that is in cheese

➢ **Gelatin** – from animals, a popular product found especially in jellies and desserts

Additional common hidden ingredients from animals include:

➢ Cochineal
➢ Isinglass
➢ Muristic acid
➢ Oleic acid
➢ Palmitic acid
➢ Pancreatin
➢ Pepsin

Most of these ingredients are usually used as additives in food.

Ingredients Which Could Be From Animals

The below ingredients serve different purposes when using them in food. Some are considered additives and others combine foods and supply extra fats. Still, just because it sounds like an animal ingredient, does not necessary mean that it is. Some are synthetically manufactured or come from plants.

They include:

- ✓ Emulsifying agents
- ✓ Fatty acid
- ✓ Adipic acid
- ✓ Glyceride
- ✓ Glycerol
- ✓ Capric acid
- ✓ Lactic acid
- ✓ Magnesium stearate
- ✓ Monoglyceride
- ✓ Anything listed as "natural flavoring"
- ✓ Clarifying agents
- ✓ Disodium inosinate
- ✓ Glyceride

- ✓ Glycerol
- ✓ Stearic acid
- ✓ Diglyceride
- ✓ Polysorbate
- ✓ Sodium stearoyl lactylate

They all have different purposes in the foods we eat, even the foods we don't think to consider. Again, if you want to live a truly Vegan way of life, it is worth taking the added step to determine if your favorite foods use the animal varieties of these ingredients.

It is imperative to recognize that the ingredients mentioned here can be found in nearly everything. It can get overwhelming, so don't drive yourself crazy. It is key to find a balance between wanting to be a strict Vegan and living a fulfilling life. If you go crazy looking things up all day long, it could affect your health in a negative way from the stress. Just do your best, and leave it at that. You are on your way to being healthy anyway.

Being a Vegan is absolutely a lifestyle commitment. Learning about the foods you eat, how to make Vegan-friendly replacements when baking and cooking, and the ingredients you may should avoid are all a part of taking on the Vegan lifestyle.

Chapter 2: Setting Up Your Vegan Food Cupboard

Setting up your food cupboard is an important step to easily creating meals on a whim. For those of you who have been vegetarians all your lives, setting up the food cupboard will be much easier. If you have only recently switch to Vegan, you will need to start from scratch. You will probably have some ingredients on hand, but all of your food cupboard needs to be Vegan friendly.

It goes without saying that the list will not include perishable items like fruits and vegetables.

Step 1: Taking an Inventory

The initial step you will take in building a Vegan food cupboard is to take an inventory of what you already have. This step is generally for those who have only just become Vegans. Yet, if you have been Vegan for a while now, you will also profit from this step. Your main goal here is to go through and ponder everything you currently have and decide if it supports the Vegan way of life.

You will also want to look at the ingredients lists of all your pre-packaged foods to determine if any of the hidden ingredients listed in the previous chapter are present. Even if you have been a practicing Vegan for a while, you may still locate some foods in your food cupboard which should not be there.

If you do find a lot of food that you need to get rid of and is unopened, do not throw away. Instead, donate them to a local food pantry. It's great to give back when and where you can!

Step 2: Stock the Essentials

It is not necessary to have a huge food cupboard complete with loads of ingredients and pre-packaged foods. All you need are the things that are important to you. If you do not bake often, for instance, do not buy baking goods until you really need them. If you love cereal, you can keep nut milk, soy milk, rice milk, and extra cereal in your food cupboard so that you don't need to run out to the store often.

When you figure out what you really need to keep on hand and what your preferences are, then you can start purchasing these things to put in your food cupboard. If you do not take this extra time, you will end up purchasing things you won't eat. Simply stock the basics, and if you need other things, you can buy them as you go along.

Step 3: Purchase Extras

It can be quite costly to stock your food cupboard all at once. There are some ingredients that you might only need once in a while. It is not imperative to buy extras at first. You can add to your food cupboard steadily as you go shopping.

Over-all, it is good to have ingredients available in order to prepare a few simple meals like pasta dishes, soups, and grain and legume dinners such as rice and beans. Consider the types of foods you eat regularly and buy the extra ingredients to have them on hand.

If you're on a tight budget, you can take care of these items as you go along. Plan your meals in advance by writing out a shopping list.

Examples of Food Cupboard Items

Although food cupboards can differ from household to household, it is helpful to see a sample food cupboard. Use this as a starting point when deciding how to stock yours, or you can simply take this list to the store and start shopping!

It will help to think of your food cupboard in terms of groupings like breakfast items, snacks, etc. Here is a rough list:

Breakfast Items
- Whole grain hot cereals such as oatmeal or cream of wheat
- Cold cereals to eat with soy milk, nut milk, or rice milk
- Vegan friendly pancake mixes
- Vegan baked goods such as muffins

Snacks
- A variety of healthy snack items such as granola bars
- Vegan treats such as cookies and cakes
- Crackers and other baked items

Miscellaneous
- Nut milk, soy milk, rice milk, and tofu in special packaging to help it store in the pantry and stay fresh longer
- Canned soups, soup mixes, and other boxed meal products such as Vegan macaroni and cheese
- Nuts and seeds such as almonds, sesame seeds, sunflower seeds, and pecans.

- ➢ Pasta – look for whole wheat varieties
- ➢ Items like spaghetti sauce, capers, pickles, extra ketchup, salad dressings, etc.

Grain Products

Here are just a few examples.

- ➢ Whole wheat rice
- ➢ Buckwheat flour
- ➢ Wheat flour
- ➢ Quinoa

Condiments

- ➢ One vegetable oil to cook with
- ➢ At least one kind of flavorful oil such as cold pressed olive oil or roasted sesame oil
- ➢ Tamara and/ or soy sauce
- ➢ Vinegar – you can keep several kinds on hand such as balsamic, rice wine, and red wine vinegar
- ➢ Salt, pepper, and herbs and spices

Baking Items

- ➢ Leavening agents such as yeast, baking powder, and baking soda
- ➢ Vegan friendly egg substitute
- ➢ Different kinds of flours

➢ Sugars and other sweetener products such as maple syrup and rice syrup

This list is designed to be a starting point. It is nearly impossible to come up with a full list due to the fact that everyone's food preferences vary so much.

Chapter 3: Vegan Cooking Basics

We now know some of the common ingredients that are used in Vegan foods. We've learned how to stock your food cupboard and find hidden ingredients in foods that Vegans should not eat.

The next step is to learn how to cook Vegan.

Now, if you already know how to cook well, you can skip this chapter altogether. However, it may be beneficial to read it anyway since there could be information you don't already know.

It is always a good idea to check around your area to see if you can find any Vegan cooking classes. They can give you a good introduction to various techniques. It can be fun learning in a group environment.

Here is we will learn:

- ✓ Setting up your kitchen
- ✓ How to follow a recipe
- ✓ Basic cooking techniques

We are going to go over some of the basic techniques. If you want to learn more, you should probably consider enrolling in a class.

Setting Up Your Kitchen

After having a well-stocked food cupboard, you need to learn to have a well-equipped kitchen to cook in.

There are 2 types of cooks - those who like to use a lot of gadgets, and those who don't. Most home cooks tend to fall somewhere in between.

Below is a list of most of the basic supplies you will need to have on hand. If you need some type of specialized equipment, you can either buy or borrow it.

- ✓ A good set of knives that include a bread knife and a chef's knife. Unless they are serrated, make sure you keep them sharp. You'll also want a large cutting board.

- ✓ An electric mixer. If you do a lot of baking, you may want to find an upright mixer that sits on your countertop.

- ✓ Various utensils such as a pair of sturdy tongs, a sieve, wooden spoons, rubber spatulas, and a sturdy wire whisk.

- ✓ A small toaster oven and a microwave

- ✓ A blender and/or a food processor.

- ✓ Optional, but nice to have on hand – a submersion mixer, crockpot, ice cream maker, a bread maker if you can't do without fresh baked bread

- ✓ A good variety of pots, pans, baking dishes, and mixing bowls.

You'll start to know what you need most after a few meals and then you can purchase the required items.

How to Follow Recipes

Learning how to follow a recipe is very important. Most recipes are easy and straightforward, but you must follow pretty precisely to avoid a bad meal.

If you are just learning to cook, you will be following recipes for quite a while. Though, as you get more comfortable in the kitchen, you will increasingly lose your dependence on them.

After you follow a few recipes, you can begin to tweak them to fit your likes and write your own original dishes down.

Basic Cooking Techniques

Once you have set up your kitchen and you understand how to follow a recipe, you will want to learn some basic cooking techniques. Below is a short list of some of the things you'll need to learn:

Learn to Use Your Knives Correctly

Know that there is a right and a wrong way to chop. Most folks don't really think much about it, but an incorrect technique can get you injured. Learning to use your knives correctly will save you a lot of headaches in the long run. And, always make sure your knives are sharp. Believe it or not, it's actually more dangerous if they're dull.

If you are not interested in taking cooking classes to learn proper chopping technique, you can watch a cooking show on television and mimic what they do.

It is pretty crucial to have a high quality chef's knife. It just makes cooking so much easier. When preparing certain foods, such as salads and soups, a lot of your time is spent chopping. If you learn how to be proficient, you can save a lot of time.

Know the Differences between Boiling, Heating and Simmering

Boiling, heating and simmering are 3 basic cooking techniques for the stove top. Boiling is when you set the heat on high and wait for the mixture to bubble. Heating is when you let it get hot but not boiling. Simmering consists

43

of putting it on low heat for a long amount of time. Things like soups and stews, for instance, are usually simmered.

Know the Difference between Baking and Broiling

In cooking, the terms "baking" and "broiling" aren't the same. Though, some things that are baked can also be broiled and vice versa. Baking occurs at a lower heat than broiling. Typical foods that are baked include breads, cookies, cakes, and flavorful dishes like vegetarian lasagna or roasted vegetables. So, food such as vegetarian lasagna, for instance, can also be broiled.

Most all ovens are equipped with a broiler, but each one is different. You will need to read your manual to learn how to work yours.

Learn How to Use Your Appliances

An additional vital step to making Vegan dishes is to be sure that you understand how to use your appliances. For instance, some don't even know it, but many microwaves also have a convection oven setting.

Common Cooking Terms and What They Mean

Once you are familiar with your kitchen and begin making recipes, you will undoubtedly come across terms that you are not familiar with. Here are some common ones you might come across:

➢ **Mash**

You can either mash with your fork if it is a smaller portion or a masher tool. Some people prefer to whip things that are normally mashed such as potatoes or squash.

➢ **Whip**

You can use a hand mixer, upright mixer, or a wire whisk to whip just about anything.

➢ **Crush**

You can crush things with the back of your knife, the bottom of a glass, or other heavy objects. There are also special kitchen gadgets used for crushing.

➢ **Grate**

Graters come in different forms, just take your pick. If you need to grate an orange peel or lemon peel, a small hand-held grater is best.

➤ **Knife Techniques**

There are several different kinds of knife techniques you can do including chop, julienne (match stick sized pieces), crush, and slice.

➤ **Blend**

Depending on what you are blending you have three choices – a regular blender, a hand-held submersion blender which works best for soups, and a food processor. The tool you use will depend on the recipe.

➤ **Puree**

When a recipe tells you to puree something, you can do it in small batches in the regular blender, use a submersion blender, or use the food processor.

A good, comprehensive cookbook will help you define any other terms you need to learn. Or, you can always search online.

Chapter 4: Making a Complete Meal

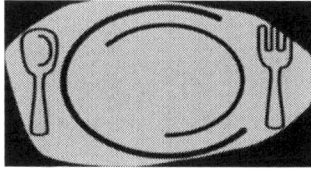

Keep in mind that simply because someone eats Vegan doesn't necessary mean that they will be naturally thin and super healthy, although the odds ARE better when living this lifestyle. However, it is still very possible to eat too many calories, even when eating Vegan, notwithstanding the wealth of nutrient dense foods to choose from. So, you still need to make your best effort to create balanced meals.

This can be a challenge at times, particularly if you are newly starting out as a Vegan. One reason is that certain vitamins and minerals, like Vitamin B12 and Iron, are more easily found in meat products. Also, Iron is more freely absorbed in the body when combined with meat.

Nutritional Considerations

Now we will discuss some of the challenges Vegans are faced with when putting meals together. This section is intended to assist you in creating healthy and balanced meal combinations which will leave you full of energy and in good health. If you are looking to lose weight or stay thin, just make sure not to consume too many calories.

Getting Adequate Protein

Vegans must get their protein from plant sources. Luckily, there are many things in the plant world that are still rich in protein:

- ➢ Soy products
- ➢ Nuts, seeds, nut milk, and nut butters
- ➢ Grains, especially quinoa
- ➢ Legumes such as kidney beans. Remember to eat a serving of grain at the same meal to make

You can also drink a serving or two of a protein drink every day. But, make sure it indicates that it is Vegan friendly. A common ingredient in a lot of protein powders is whey, which is a derivative of milk.

Getting Enough Iron

For women, getting enough iron is a challenge in and of itself, but for a Vegan, it's that much harder. As a matter of fact, many Vegans are diagnosed with iron deficiencies if they do not ensure that they get enough. You may want to consult your doctor to get suggestions for an iron supplement. You can get plant-based, Vegan-friendly iron supplements at the health food store. Also, you can eat these iron rich foods:

- ✓ Spinach
- ✓ Green beans
- ✓ Brewer's yeast (a supplement)
- ✓ Wheat germ
- ✓ Lima beans
- ✓ Dried fruit such as raisins and prunes
- ✓ Cooking in a cast iron skillet
- ✓ Blackstrap molasses (use in baking or take as a supplement)

Note: To make plant protein more absorbable, couple it with a Vitamin C rich food, drink, or supplement. For instance, you can have a small glass of orange juice with a meal which contains a lot of iron.

Eat Foods Rich in Vitamin B

Vegans normally get enough Vitamin B since grains are a good source. But, Vitamin B 12 is a little more challenging. You can supplement with a Vegan-friendly version of B 12 which is often synthetic. Also, some cereals and drinks can contain Vitamin B 12.

Getting Plenty of Calcium

Thanks to fortification, it is easy for a Vegan to get their calcium. Below are some foods to consume:

- ✓ Soy milk, nut milks, and rice milks are often fortified with calcium. Make sure the product is Vegan friendly and contains a good amount of calcium.

- ✓ Nuts, such as hazelnuts and almonds.

- ✓ Leafy green veggies and other vegetables such as bok choy, collard greens, turnip greens, and okra are also rich in calcium.

When preparing vegetables, if you choose to boil them, drink the water. A lot of the calcium leaves the food during the cooking process and ends up in the water.

Getting it Right

If you have been a practicing Vegan for a while, you probably already have the hang of this. If not, you will want to plan some of your meals out in advance until you get the hang of it. Even if you have been a Vegan for a while, it is still a good idea to occasionally take a step back and plan a few meals. Not only will this help assure that you get the nutrients you need, but it helps build variation since you are planning meals with new ingredients.

You can also keep a food journal. Keep track of what you eat, how you cooked it, whether or not you liked it, and if you would alter anything. This is a good way to see if you are getting the correct nutrients. Don't analyze it too deeply though. Just make sure you're getting what you need.

You can also take a multivitamin addition to eating a healthy diet.

Vegan-Friendly Ethnic Cuisine

There are many ethnic cuisines that are vegetarian. As a result, they have many tasty Vegan dishes to enjoy when eating out or getting take out. This allow for a diet with much-needed variety.

Below is a short list of some of the cuisines you can enjoy. Most of these also have meat dishes, but their vegetarian options are very tasty.

- Indian

  There are plenty of grain and vegetable based options.

- Chinese

  Buddhist monks eat a largely vegetarian diet.

- French

  Fresh fruits and vegetables form the centerpiece of this Mediterranean cuisine.

- Italian

  Italian food also focuses on fresh fruits and vegetables

- Korean

  Lots of rice and vegetables are consumed on a daily basis.

- Thai

  Much like traditional, produce based Chinese food, Thai also packs some heat.

- Vietnamese

  Asian cuisine uses a lot of plant-based foods.

- ➢ **Greek**

  Another Mediterranean region cuisine that features a lot of fresh produce.

This list is by no means complete. For instance, Mediterranean cuisine is Vegan friendly because there are many dishes that focus on plant-based foods. There are a lot of countries that make up that region including France, Italy, Greece, Spain, Morocco, and Algeria.

Asian cuisine also has a lot of dishes that are made chiefly from plant-based foods. Even if a recipe calls for meat, you can easily leave it out without ruining the flavor.

Chapter 5: Special Nutritional Considerations

The Vegan diet is ideal for attaining good health if you pay attention to your calories and create better, more complete nutritional meals.

However, many people have other health problems to be concerned with. Some use the Vegan diet to help them restore their health.

Below is a list of some common illnesses and how to alter your Vegan diet to accommodate. Keep in mind that the Vegan diet is a healthy diet to start with, so it makes these adjustments a lot easier.

Diabetes

There are 2 types of diabetes – Type 1, which people are born with, and Type 2, which comes later in life. The Vegan diet, particularly a low-fat one, is specifically useful for people who have Type 2 diabetes. However, Type 1 sufferers can also profit.

If you stick to low-fat foods, whole grains, legumes, nuts, seeds, and plenty of fruits and vegetables, it will help manage your condition naturally as long as you take any prescribed medication in addition. Because your body cannot produce enough insulin, there's no other way to get it without the medication.

Diseases of the Circulatory System

Diseases of the circulatory system, like high cholesterol, high blood pressure, and generalized heart disease, all benefit from the Vegan diet. This is due to the fact that it is low in fat and cholesterol.

Low Fat Diet

The Vegan diet is certainly low in fat. In fact, since you are not consuming meat, it is low in saturated fat and high in the good fats which come from avocado, nuts and seeds, and several oils.

Nevertheless, there are things to keep in mind. First, keep away from trans fats. They can be even worse for you than saturated fats. You can get what you need by eating coconut every once in a while. You can also cook with coconut oil, which could be a substitute for butter or lard.

Low Sugar Cooking

If you follow the Vegan diet as it is meant to be followed, it is naturally low in sugar. Though, just like with any routine, there is a possibility that you can overdo it. Your body requires some sugar, which you obtain naturally from fresh and dried fruits as well as maple syrup, sugar cane, or rice syrup.

There are also baked goods and other sugary foods available (such as Vegan-friendly chocolate) which can be just as addictive as their non-Vegan equivalents. Moderation is always key. If you want or need to follow a low-sugar diet, train your body to appreciate sugar in its natural state in fruit, and not baked goods.

LOW SODIUM COOKING

People who follow the Vegan diet are just as disposed to too much sodium as anyone else. Followed in its purest state, the Vegan diet is low in sodium, but reach for the salt shaker too often and it can affect your health.

Gluten-Free Cooking

It may seem like a challenge to do away with gluten on a Vegan diet. Know that it is very possible. If you need or want to avoid gluten, below is a short list of some of the grains to avoid:

> Oats
> Barley
> Wheat
> Rye
> Kamut
> Spelt

There are still quite a few grains and starches that you can eat:

> Rice, especially brown rice
> Quinoa
> Corn
> Millet
> Potatoes

Simply follow the Vegan diet as you typically would but only consume the grains which don't produce gluten.

You can definitely acclimate the Vegan diet to help with an assortment of health problems. That's what makes it so popular.

Chapter 6: Recipes

Recipes

Now, it's time for you to put it all together and try some new recipes. This section gives you a selection of some recipes you can make on your Vegan diet journey. Feel free to adjust and change them as you would like.

Try to keep a cooking journal so you can keep track of what you like. That way, if you prepare something you like, you can repeat it.

Appetizers

Bruschetta

A common Italian dish which is great as an appetizer or snack. It is naturally Vegan.

Ingredients:

¼ cup scallions, chopped

1 large tomato, diced

1 clove garlic, minced

1 tablespoon dried basil

6 slices fresh, whole grain bakery bread

Olive oil

Instructions:

Preheat oven to 350 degrees. In a small mixing bowl, combine first four ingredients. Spray a baking sheet with nonstick cooking spray and arrange bread sliced on sheet. Spoon tomato mixture evenly over all four slices. Drizzle with olive oil. Bake for about 15 minutes, or until bread is toasted.

Black Olive Hummus

Hummus is a typical vegetarian food that is low in fat and high in protein. Spread on whole grain, Vegan crackers or serve with bread.

Ingredients:

1, 15 oz can cooked chickpeas, drained and rinsed
1 tablespoon water
1/3 cup fresh lemon juice
1/4 cup pitted black olives, diced

Instructions:

Combine all of the ingredients in a food processor or blender and pulse until creamy. Transfer to a serving dish and serve with crackers, bread, or whole grain pita wedges.

Soups

Greek Style Chickpea Soup

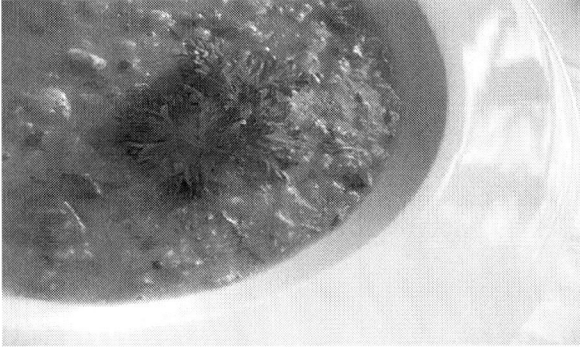

This is an example of a robust Greek dish that is Vegan friendly. Serve with slices of fresh, whole grain bread and a salad.

Ingredients:

3, 15 ounce cans of chickpeas, drained and rinsed

1 large onion, chopped

1 teaspoon dried rosemary

3 tablespoons fresh, chopped parsley

1 teaspoon sea salt

4 cloves garlic, chopped fine

1, 28 ounce can crushed tomatoes (keep the juice)

3 cups water

2 tablespoons olive oil

Salt and pepper to taste

Instructions:

Add all of the ingredients to a large pot. Bring to a boil, then simmer on low for an hour until flavors are well blended. You can also cook it in a crock pot on the low setting for 4-6 hours.

Classic Minestrone Soup

This is an all-time favourite. The nice thing about it is that you can use whichever vegetables you have on hand.

Ingredients:

2 large carrots, peeled and chopped

3 celery stalks, chopped

1 medium onion, chopped

2 cloves garlic, minced

2 zucchini, chopped

1 cup broccoli florets

1 cup spinach leaves

1 can crushed tomatoes

1 cup canned kidney beans, rinsed

8 cups water

1 cup small pasta like elbows or orzo

salt and pepper to taste

Fresh chopped parsley for a garnish

Instructions:

Combine all of the ingredients except the pasta in a soup pot. Bring to a boil and then simmer for at least one hour until the vegetables are soft. Add pasta during the last fifteen minutes of cooking and cook for eight to ten minutes. You can also cook the soup in the crock pot. Just add all of the ingredients at once.

Salads

Vegan Cesar Salad

The Cesar salad is a classic but the dressing is definitely not Vegan friendly. This recipe fixes that.

Ingredients for the Dressing:

1/2 cup Vegan mayonnaise

1/2 cup brewer's yeast

Juice of 1 lemon

2 teaspoons cracked pepper

Ingredients for the Salad:

4 Cups of Torn Romaine Lettuce Leaves

1 Cup of Black Olives - chopped

3 tablespoons of Grated Soy Parmesan

Instructions:

At the bottom of a large salad bowl, whisk all of the salad dressing ingredients together. Toss in the romaine lettuce until dressing is well coated. Top with black olives and parmesan cheese and serve.

Classic Salad

The classic salad is, of course, Vegan friendly. Simply choose the vegetables that you desire and the dressing that you desire, as long as it is Vegan. You can make your own Vegan dressings easily. Vinaigrettes are particularly easy because all they entail is equal parts of oil and vinegar stirred together. You can also add salt, pepper, and spices to taste.

Salads are great because they are easy and you can use whatever you have in the house. Keep your fridge well stocked with produce and you can make a healthy salad whenever you want.

Main Courses

Vegan Lentil Tacos

Lentils make a nice substitute for the traditional beef that usually goes in tacos.

Ingredients:

1 cup dried, brown lentils

1, 8 ounce can of tomato sauce

1 packet taco seasoning mix (Vegan)

Corn tortillas or taco shells

Shredded romaine lettuce

Cucumber slices

Chopped, fresh tomatoes

Guacamole

Salsa

Soy Sour Cream

Instructions:

Soak lentils in a large bowl until soft, approximately one hour. Transfer to a saucepan and blend with tomato sauce and taco seasoning. Add roughly ¼ cup of water. Simmer on low until heated. Spoon into taco shells or tortillas and top with things such as sour cream, salsa, lettuce, cucumber, and tomato.

Healthy Vegetable Casserole

Casseroles are another healthy option for Vegans. The good thing about them is once you have the recipe down, you can make tons of substitutions.

Ingredients:

1 cup cooked brown rice

1, 8 ounce can of tomato soup

1, 8 ounce can legumes such as chick peas or kidney beans

4 cups vegetables of choice – try zucchini, mushrooms, carrots, celery, eggplant, tomatoes, leeks, onions, garlic, and potatoes

Instructions:

Spray a medium casserole dish with nonstick cooking spray. Layer with brown rice. Add vegetables on top of the rice. You can mix the vegetables together, choose one type of vegetable, or layer different kinds – it's up to you. Pour soup over vegetables. Cover and bake at 350 degrees for 45 minutes.

Side Dishes

When it comes to side dishes, there are many options you can try. Below are some ideas:

➢ Cover a baking sheet with vegetables such as carrots, zucchini, eggplant, asparagus, and parsnips. Sprinkle with olive oil, salt, and paper and bake at 400 degrees until soft.

➢ You can add water or vegetable stock to cooked squash, cauliflower, or potatoes and mash or whip. Use salt and pepper to taste. Miso broth works especially well.

➢ Serve a nice salad as a side dish, or sticks of fresh vegetables.

➢ Choose your favorite grain, such as quinoa, millet, or couscous and prepare according to the package directions. Season with salt and pepper and serve with your main course. You can also add vegetables and herbs to give it more nutritional value.

➢ Don't forget pickled vegetables – these make a nice alternative to standard side dishes.

Use your imagination. You can also serve fruit as a side dish, or Vegan apple sauce.

Desserts

Vegan Brownies

It is vital to be sure that all of the ingredients are Vegan friendly. Yes, you can get Vegan chocolate!

Ingredients:

1 cup white flour

1 cup whole wheat flour

1 cup water

1 cup brown sugar

1 teaspoon salt

1 teaspoon vanilla extract

¾ cup cocoa powder for baking

½ cup vegetable oil

½ teaspoon baking powder

Optional: ½ - 1 cup chopped nuts, ½ - 1 cup chocolate chips

Instructions:

Spray a 9 x 13 baking sheet with nonstick cooking spray. Combine flour, water, brown sugar, and salt. (A wire whisk works best). Stir in vanilla extract, coco powder, vegetable oil, and baking powder using a wooden spoon. Spread evenly into the baking sheet and bake at 400 for about 30 minutes, until a toothpick inserted on the sides comes out clean

Some Things You Can Do With Fresh Fruit

Seasonal fresh fruit is a great dessert. You can eat it as is or try any of these options:

- ✓ Make a fresh fruit salad with your favorite seasonal fruits. Season the salad with citrus juice.

- ✓ Top fresh fruit with vanilla soy yogurt

- ✓ Add fresh fruit such as chopped apple to a small baking dish. Top with walnuts, brown sugar, and cinnamon and bake at 350 until apples are soft.

✓ Do the same as above, but try pears, peaches, blueberries or different varieties of apples instead. You can also experiment with the nuts and the spices. This makes a nice replacement for apple, pear, blueberry, or peach cobbler or crisp.

✓ Grill fresh pineapple slices or bananas. Slice the banana in half cross wise and sprinkle with cinnamon.

Use your imagination. If you heat your fruit in any way, it can be a rich and satisfying dessert.

Conclusion

Whether you have been Vegan for a quite while or are just starting out, you should now have a more complete understanding of what it means to be Vegan. This includes:

- ✓ How to stock your pantry

- ✓ Hidden ingredients to avoid

- ✓ An understanding of basic cooking techniques

- ✓ Typical foods that make up a Vegan diet

- ✓ How to put together healthy meals

- ✓ Adapting the Vegan diet for different health problems

- ✓ Some new recipes

No matter the reason that you chose the Vegan way of life, this book has been intended as a source to get you closer to attaining a completely Vegan and healthy lifestyle.

So, what now?

The Vegan way of life embodies a pledge to bettering your health. In addition, it is a socially conscious decision for many people. If you want to better your impact on the environment, eat local foods whenever you can and buy organic. Also, try to stay away from genetically modified foods.

The Vegan way of life can positively better your health. It is much easier in the Vegan diet to make healthy choices.

Printed in Great Britain
by Amazon